Eve
A River Flowing

POEMS

Jane Bauer

NEWMAN SPRINGS PUBLISHING
320 Broad Street
Red Bank, NJ 07701

First originally published by Newman Springs Publishing 2024

ISBN 979-8-88763-589-7 (Paperback)
ISBN 979-8-88763-590-3 (Digital)

Printed in the United States of America

The Poems

Introductory Poem
Eve—a River Flowing

"Eve"—a river flowing through creation.
Flowing over hills and desert sands,
with dry arid land, sifting through rugged farmer's hand.
Flowing and nourishing bird and beast, earth and tree.

Her life-giving flow, this sacred river, in our depths we already know.
Her presents bringing water from snowy mountain peaks, to wide open seas.
Her force moving from stormy skies above, trickling and gathering, racing and loving, hard and fast, across this vast open land.

Feeding all at hand, with her joy of creation and man.
Feeding the earth, giving worth to everything in need.
Awakening dormant sleeping seeds.
Seeds waiting to burst forth and finally breath.

Sprouting, stretching, pushing, being.
Bringing life, bringing fruits for all.
Both bird and beast.
Her nourishing embrace, bringing wild sprawling feasts.

Her endless journey, from mighty mountain peaks, flowing to turquoise ocean deeps.
Her power tumbling, over mountain rock and boulder.
Passing all that stand, to look in wonder.
Flowing, dancing, swirling, birthing, bringing forth life from land and birthing man.

Birthing life of land and life for men.
To stand true and proud before God and to know…
That all is good.

Chapter 1

Eve's Crisis

What Is a Woman? (Who Is She Really?)

What is a woman?
A question asked and caused a commotion.
Do we really have a clue or a notion of her full power and dimension?

In a time of gender fluidity, gender bending and twisting,
creating new listings of pronouns nowhere to be found.
Can't be explained from where this all came.
Never known or heard before.

Creating new concepts, soaked in threats.
Don't ask questions.
Just accept!

She "a woman," it's just a social concept.
"A woman," a social construction.
Apparently…a kind of obstruction.

So what is next?

Where are these ideas sprouting from?
What force has created them?
What mind has mined and drilled for such thoughts that try to kill
the source of where we hail?

As our mother earth struggles with us and our abuses and deals with
our obtuseness.
We start to further dismantle our human mother.

You know—"the woman," the birth giver.
Or, should I say, "The birthing person!"
What an offence to our Creator.
Without her, you would not be here.

The creative force created man and woman in the garden.
Male and female, man and woman, hand in hand to walk this land,
equal in value but different in role…
She to stroll through valley of conception and birth and he to roam
and hunt and provide for the young life that has sprung from his
wife, and he shall provide safety and shelter for all.

Well…as for the woman, who is the subject of this poem.
She gave us all life.
Like a timeless *river flowing* through creation…
The woman, who even went under the knife and risked her own life
to Grace us with ours…
Can we appreciate her prowess and power?

She conceives of us. She receives us from the spring of life.
She allows us to spring from her loins.
She nurtures and loves and gives life.
She cradles and soothes us in her belly day and night.
Till we burst into this life, helped by a midwife.
She nurses, sings, and brings us good things, that our needs are eased
and quieted, and we can set forth into the world wise enough…to
be…as good as she.

But when does life begin?
Let's introduce another social construction.
Let's say, life begins where it's convenient for all our whims.
Let's say, life begins when our own conscience kicks in.
Let's say, let's create an artificial social concept
that allows us to destroy and destruct what is inconvenient.

So the unborn life, which comes "unplanned," can be with no conscience, happily abandoned.
Ripped from the sacred place, from the "mother," "the womb," that other social construction.
That woman with life-giving womb.
The womb of life, when under the surgeon's knife, becomes a tomb of death, for both social concepts.

"Woman" and "life" brought under the social deconstructing knife.
Creating mass confusion with sex and gender delusion(?).

When we take God's creation, the "divine mother" and the youngest most innocent of our
"tribal structure,"
and tell them they are dispensable, destructible, and disposable.
Then I can only conclude, we as a people have allowed ourselves to embrace false freedom and, consequently, destructively become so corruptible.

And this is our own epitaph on the hill of creation.
Our own crime, which will lay dormant in time and haunt us *all*... forever.

Confusing Times

Confusing times, bringing people to their needs.
Screaming out for guidance and clarity.
The nation falling to its knees.

The Information Age.
This sea of digital waves.
Everything accessible,
oh so much possible.
The smothering races, gasping for breath,
in the digital depths.
Drowning in their own confusion.
Leading to mass delusion.

Human beings stripped by hand.
Stripped of their motherland.
Now cocooned in a new digital womb.
A womb so tight,
it squeezes the life and breath from all.

Separated from one another,
sister and brother, longing for each other.
This digital space pulsating,
the impulses shaking,
mankind's foundation.

This new playing field allows no seed for…
Feeling the soft breeze over Mother Earth's falling leaves.

It allows no seed for…
blustery walks against wind and hail.
Beating the skin till it's pale and numb,
till you are soaked through,
It allows no seed for…you!

We must be free, to breathe and be,
Live and love, caress the earth,
Embrace the sky and return to our true…Maternal ties.
A wound of old and new, a muse to light and guide the true.
Back to the mother… not this digital imposter in lieu.
Return to tree and land.
Digging and planting with respectful hand.
Loving bird and beast.
Respecting all indeed.
Caressing and accepting each other as sister and brother.
As we follow God's lead.

With speed, humanity reclaims all that it needs,
to create a home, where Love and Decency,
are the main priority.
Sending this digital plain back to where it came,
rejecting all insane, who claim it's all the same.

The divine shines a light to cripple this digital might.
And brings us back to our senses.
Repeat this sentence.

I return to my senses…
I return to my senses…
I return to my senses…

The Crown of Light

Our world has stopped, all forced to stop living,
forced to stop running, like headless chickens,
not knowing where we are going and why.

The earth still spinning, still breathing, still needing.
Shaking herself to find balance and strength.
The seas scattered plastic, twisted through generations of us.

Life from beyond, plunges into the depths,
shining a light for us all.
These loving waves, pulsating the loins of the land.

This fiery wreath, wrapping around ancient pains and all trauma at
hand.
Challenging all that is with her renewed breath.
The breath of old dying away.
The crowns pulsating rebirth.
God-given flow
to a
New Earth.

The Golden Shoes

"I like your golden shoes," the son says, passing his mother.
Her thoughts fleeting, one to another.
What of it all, the blame, seemingly always the same.
Who did it? Who done it?
The recognition…the shame.

The tired gray rain, racing down the windowpane.
Refreshingly simple, but perhaps a little mundane.
But mundane causes no trouble, it doesn't rock the boat
and insist on execution.

The executed heads piled high.
What's the point? "Whatever"…by the by.

The queen insisted on it.
The queen of broken hearts.
The chaos caused by few and it all for a pair of…
…golden shoes.

Please, God, Help the Madness

Please, God, help the madness; it is spiraling out of control.
The silver screen has darkened now, and we don't know where to go.

We've been following it for many years, leaving field and tree behind.
But now we are on rocky ground, and we don't know how to find.

How to find our way back home, from the desolate place.
You see it in the emptiness and lostness…Children's face.

Please, God, send us a new plan of precisely where to go.
Our tribe has wandered off the track and has lost its godly "sole."

The earth has trembled, the sea gone cold.
The mountains point to another world.

People, wipe your eyes anew; remember your godliness.
Free your ears of poison food,
with mountain breeze and nature bless.

Then look upon the mountaintop,
the snowy peaks, the flying flocks.

Perhaps indeed will this cleanse thee,
of lostness and of peril.
I hope to God,
it comes to pass and that we do not…perish.

Race

I woke up this morning with race in my head.
I mean, I'm hardly out of bed, and this stuff is racing around my head.
Every day, I see it pouring out of the TV set.
All over the Internet.
"America is racist."

I hear a poetry slam.
About a black man and gang drive-by shootings,
And underground crime rings.

But what's the solution?

They blame the white man for his grand plan,
of plantations and girls and boys in chains.
White privilege…whatever that means!

I get it, the ghettos soaked in drugs and gang crime,
but it has nothing to do with me or mine.
But I feel it, their pain, the blame, this has to change.

But the problem is not your white friend or the guy you think has too much to spend.

Why not look at the institutions that divide us from each other?
Turning White brother against Black brother.
Look at the drugs that turn Black brother against Black brother.
Look at what took black Mamas and Papas from Baptist church pews…to the ghettos.

Look at what took Mamas and Papas from singing songs of praise to God above…to sitting in a haze of "fake love."
Fake love, in the form of a pipe, that takes the love and life from you and everyone else too!

Look at the moral deprivation and degradation pouring out of the Internet, as your kids sit and eat what they can get.
Looking for goodness and grace but faced with Cardi B's butt shaking it up.
Is this the food for our generation—the glue to hold us as a nation?
Cardi B, Stallion Thee, crackpots, gunshots.
Desperate Black men running from cops.
To escape from what?

Claim back your soulful blackness.
Burn up the toxic drug culture that has punctured our lives.
Stand again as generations before, gathering on church floors.
Singing and dancing, a community standing together as one.
God's praise singing and swaying in the air…protecting the babies to come.
Woman and man, hand in hand, loving each other, forgetting the trouble that was.
Families together, communities forever.
Tight and strong.
Swaying in harmony to the preacher's song.

Free from chains of plantations.
Free from chains of gun violence.
Free the young man gone wrong, gone astray, in a haze of some poison.
That has taken every notion and emotion he has.

Free from chains of ignorance that stopped him seeing where his path was.
Free at last…
Free at last…

Finally… Free at last…

(W)Rap It Up, Enough Is Enough

Wrap it up, enough is enough.
Pornography at a finger's touch.
Much too much!
Children's fingers being burned.
So not earned.
The pain going deep.
Really, no one can sleep.
Scarred and scared for the lives,
so badly, they want to go under the knife.
Boy or girl, I don't know.
So many choices, where to go?
I can't feel.
Who am I?
What am I?
So unclear.
All the fear!

And what of Cardi B and Stallion Thee,
Sold out to the biggest dollar…I feel.

What a killer, culture dying.
Women crying, losing their man to some striptease trend.

Family life, also under the knife.
Moneymaking machines,
Slicing and dicing our DNA and genes.

Is it all just to make a buck?
Does no one really give a f——k?
Have we gone too far with our boundary-breaking liberal agenda?

The sixties came and went, flower power, LSD, and
music…
A season later, babies born to no home,
nowhere to go, mama too young.
Sent away and who had to pay?

Not the "Mamas and the Papas" anyway.
So "Joni" told me!

State homes filled with kids.
"Christ's brides" tending to their needs.
The Madonna's tears flowing,
She's falling to her knees.

What of the responsibility to the innocent of today?

"WAP"atiers, innocent ears, shaking it up, not knowing what's
coming
and where this is going.

And where are those who "Serve and Protect"?
Thrown to the wayside like garments of old…. No respect!

Our throwaway society will have no responsibility.
For kids and cops, corn and crops, Indian farmers bleeding,
others hardly breathing and some seed no longer seeding.

And the porn pop-culture honey-trap smothering Billy,
As it rolls down her face, telling the kids…
…Isn't this great.

What Now, My Love? (Part 1)

How to start, I know it's hard.
Just sit still, breathe in and out,
open up, release your fear, and all will become clear.

A child in need, sitting still, spiraling in confusion.
Her tears falling hard, her foundation totally scattered.
All the pieces, swirling in her emotions.
Born to a time of so much commotion.
So much of everything, but all with so little meaning.

Her young heart heavy, her wisdom craving a connection, for a time
long forgotten.
Her wise eyes scouting, schoolbooks, TikTok, modern muses, search-
ing for less confusion.

The menu of modern life, offering a diet of sensory overload and
strife.
Be happy. Do your best. All is well.
But don't forget they say "America is hell" and "the forefathers" are
responsible.

Oh my god! How should I feel with all this social self-deprecation?
"Left" versus "right," multiracial strife, gender norms under the knife.
Social norms sledgehammered until we've all had enough.
Until we fall to where there are no boundaries.
In fact, nothing left at all.

But I need norms, boundaries, and things of old.
Church bells ringing in the old town hall.
Gossiping seniors on street corners.
God's blessing caressing the nation
As it follows life's rules.

But if there are no boundaries, no morals, and no norms…
What should the foundation of my young life be built upon?
How should it be in this life you see?

God Bless America

God bless America, the God-given ship,
afloat among the great seas.
Winds high, waves crashing from all sides,
shaking the hope-beaten decks.
Beaten by long white-bearded shipbuilding visionaries.

The crew in conflict, confused, huddling below deck.
Fearing God's elements that challenge its track.
The feared hungry waves engulf the lost vessel.
Where is it headed, and how should it get there?

The crew squabble and quarrel, throw blame and dismay.
Voices load with fury, fire a blaze.
Heavy, worn, leathery wisdom-filled books,
slammed on worn old salt-eaten tables…in rage.
In search of answers to light the direction for all in this lost vessel.

Its compass a-smash, scattered among worn floor cracks.
How should it be out among the great seas?
No compass at hand,
no land to be seen, and wind ablaze with encircling waves?

The vessel fights for its life!
It is tossed and thrown, beaten and bashed.
Its sails ripped from its guts.
The treasures of generations collected by many, now tossed to the depths,
recklessly, respectlessly.

Now all seems lost.
The treasures have gone.
The innards of the ship have brought quiet to the squabbling figures
afloat.

Finally, the wild winds seize, the battling waves settle,
and before them…
Light-filled land rises on the hopeful horizon.

Chapter 2

Eve's Comfort

Church Pews (Part 2)

Some time has passed; she sits happily in her community.
The girls and boys, side by side, on church pews, singing songs of praise.
No phone bulging from teen-jean pockets.
No kids searching for clicks and hits, tidbits,
to enhance their sense of self and inner wealth.

The songs of praise spiraling,
their hearts yearning and filling anew.
Heads light, clear, and free from fear.
Eyes a-meeting, innocent with joy,
bodies a-beating in love's harmony.
Swaying to the feeling of a renewed nation.
The community's praise and prayers,
no longer delaying.

Seeking forgiveness for times of old.
Times of ignorance and violence.
That have caused the fate of the nations,
to sit in the trenches for generations.
Soldiers, guns in hand, pillaging the land.
Times of old—oh, so bold and brave,
those overfilled graves…now empty.

God's birdsong carried on the breeze,
sent to ease these wrongs.
Church bells ringing across the land,
the community battling hand in hand,
for communion, bringing light and love for a
renewed nation and…a new generation.

The Universe within Us All

The universe within us all.
Big and small, expensive blue, who would know at all,
Or dare have a clue.

Dive in deep, have no fear, perhaps all will become clear.

You may shout it into crowded halls filled with seeking minds
And pounding hearts.
Where once was bloody battleground, with battle cries echoing over
distant hills.
Or shout it to the desert heights, with the rattle of snakes in places
so dry.
Or shout it at the eternal sky, as eagle sores high on pockets invisible
to the naked eye.

The universal eye, so high and free and eternal, like the eagle eye
soaring and swooping through dust-blown Desert sky.
The eagle eye, so wise, so present, and so feared on land and wind.
The universe ly's there.

It's a spiraling Journey to eternity.
Lie on the Eagle's back and embrace the mighty flight,
As it rules over the space upon high.

And when the burning ball of Sun sinks beneath the hills, the
blackness
of eternal being embraces all that is, and all is calm and rests in the
universal nest of night.

Space–the Final Frontier

I am here, where once was called "the frontier."
Wide open spaces, with so many faces.
Rock formations, Trancing nation, Alien space invasion, Indigenous
vibration.

This land, so vast, carrying cowboy and Indian echoes
of times past.
The windblown tumbleweed terrain,
sundrenched with both beauty and pain.

The coyote howling, proud head stretching to the heavens in
reverence.
His Indian brothers, aligned to the stars.
Their souls dancing a ritual beat through the universe.

The shaman drum beating, the howling wind sweeping,
this sacred space.
Vibration through the nation.
Dog and man spiraling hand in hand through this starry land.
This land of time and space, dissolving in its place.
As Indian drums, meditative beat, naked Indian feet,
pounding on land, awakening man from a sleep of old.

A sweet sleep, a deep sleep, a cocoon, a protection.
For all man in all nation.
Vibration high, angels in the expansive sky.
Drumbeat, stomping feet, fire ablaze, chanting, swirling through
fiery haze.

This haze, to pave the way,
to clarity of mind.
For man and child…and all of its kind.
To thrive…and finally be alive.

To Walk "the Boards"

Costumes and shoes, pink and blue.
Pointy toes peeking out of long pantyhose.
A room as small as a shoebox,
bulging with all sorts of stuff.

High heels, swaying frocks, long locks, wigs for all occasions
and a long mantle for those blowy, wet, winter, grey days.
As carriages splash the streets clean.
And drainpipes flood pavements pristine.

The gray rain dripping onto metal rooftops, sounding like a symphony at dawn.
And dawn sweeping in with fiery red heels,
like a gladiator across those well-worn dramatic boards.

Those hungry ladies and lords, hordes of hungry folk,
awaiting a drama, a song, a distraction from the misery and gloom,
that doth loom on street corners.
The misery dripping like the gray rain, but no symphony here….
just pain.

Eyes wide, hearts pumping, blood red, flushed cheeks, dirty nails,
and cold feet.
Men and boys, prancing, dancing, flowery words,
seldom heard on those…
dirty street corners.

Here heaven opens as drama strikes.
Culprit with hand in knife,
cold, bold corpse lying on cold dead ground.
The crowd gets loud!

The world of dread and gloom,
Pain and shame,
left in a room very far away.
They huddle together in awe of the beauty and color afoot.
"The life on this stage doth carry us away to a place of beauty and
pain.
Laughter, love, and loss."
Swirling in this wonderful romance,
this cosmos, between performer and inspired guest.

Bringing the best forward, for both to set foot and go forth,
Into the bustling streets,
The chattering feet,
The challenges of defeat and death, birth and regret.

Knowing well that this shall all play out again and again.

And we all know it oh…so well.

Bearfoot

His bare brown weather-rugged feet walk the copper rustic sun-drenched Earth.
The copper shaded dust, aswirl in the desert sky.
The sky vast expansive blue—a blue and a vastness longed by many but seen by few.

As heaven and earth unite, he walks alone, at one with all, and all is still.
All is brother, all is mother, all is father, and all is sister.
His proud burnt brown brow aglow with the rare moisture of this arid land.

As his kin before him, he caresses his "mother" with a loving glance.
And his loving deep earth-brown eyes cast themselves to the endless blue sky,
in respect for the forever loyal Father above.

And he walks on.

 Revelation

Revelation, a chapter to sing.
The wrongs that cling to the trees.
The trees humming in the sacred breeze.
The Lord's prayers hanging in the branches,
Swaying in love's harmony.

Lovebirds in branches.
Loveless trenches, empty church benches, all fists in clenches.

Swords in the sky, Angels' wings flying high.
Battling day and night.
Fighting the fight of might and will.
On a timeless hill…of God's creation.

Love Song

A love song, to right the wrongs.
From above, soaked in God's love.
Love for man and land, hand in hand.
A birdsong, greeting the ears of man.

"Awaken, please."
Swaying on the breeze.
Eyes wide open to God's creation.
The sacred heart, embracing the nations.

Connection

The earth calls its children back.
The lost ones, they have wa(o)ndered off the track.
The trap so bright, so alluring, so tempting.

Now alone, the children pine for comfort and connection.
The mother sends a whisper on a gentle spring breeze.
The spring's blessed breeze carries her loving call with ease.
The call for her offspring.

The children huddle and restlessly wait and wonder.
They sit in the lost abyss of their own emptiness,
a long timeless slumber.

A bright spark of a child awakens to her call.
She is carried by the sweet embracing breeze…and returns.
This is union…
This is love…

Awaken, Little Ones

Awaken, little ones, the father has spoken.
The sleep must end; the spell may be broken.
He awaits your presence and un-trances the nations.

All come to the great hall, for it's time for the gathering.
It is long awaited and is now happening.
Let your light shine into the world, to those children still in a slumber.
For winter has passed.
And we must now gather.

Like springtime flowers,
Cutting through cold winter frost.
We must bring new life into the world.
Leaving the cold winter in the past.

As daffodils sway and glow in the early spring light.
We must do as they do and bring beauty renewed,
and breath of life.

Come, little ones, do as the daffodils do.
Shine, sway, glow, and awaken the world…

Out of the long winter cold.

Everest

Everest, a mighty climb,
the golden duel in the Earth's crown.
So bright and radiant.
Whiter than white.

Prayer flags sending praise to the mountaintop.
Buddhist prayer bells chiming to the loyal flocks.
Red robes swaying over loyal humble feet.
The sweat and blood of Western man, the trauma of defeat.
Young boys' heads shaved to pave the way,
for a climb to the divine.

All are striving to reach the top.
To reach the godly in the rock.
The sweat and pain of bleeding wounds, cut by cold rock and icy winds.
Ice pick slung into bitter wind and frozen rock.
Securing the way for searching souls,
longing for peace.

The radiant red robes, shaved heads, ringing bells, meditative chant,
flowing over hills,
pulsating in this Godly peak.
Western man, rugged boots, iron wills, longing to conquer the ultimate,
that reaches to the heavens,
in Reverence.

Both mountaineer and monk looking longingly,
in revere
at this Godly sphere.

Winter Blues

She walks a straight line, she walks a fine line,
awash with thoughts but…empty.
Birds in the midday sky, flying, soaring high and low, fast and slow.
She sees no pattern…just freedom.

The wind—light, mild, and moist.
The grass—soft, a bed to lay one's head, staring longingly
at the endless…blue sky.

Clouds floating by, taken by the speedy winds up on high.
And below, a gentle wind blows, tossing toasted leaves among the
green blades.
The emerald blades, adance in the comforting breeze.
The mild sun, soft and gentle, thawing the end…

…of the winter blues.

The Warm Winter Coat

The warm winter coat,
Long and brown and thick and heavy.
Wrapped around the frail figure of the young pale girl.

The warm winter coat protects, like a safe and sturdy harbor in a
night storm.
Wrapped around the frail framed girl, bringing comfort and warmth.
Like the eternal loving, safe embrace of her mother.

The warm winter coat, a close friend,
when the winter winds blow hard and cold.
A loving companion when the day is wet and gray,
and the light fights for its place in the sky.

The warm winter coat.

The Waves

The waves, layered, moving across the aquaplane.
The watery landscape dancing and soaring in the invisible wind.
Their white foamy tips crashing softly as they come to land.

The sea, so vast—future, present, and past.
Full of life and death.
Bringing life, bringing feasts of life, bringing renewed breath.

It greets the shore and retreats again.
This dance forward and backward.
Never settling too long.
Like a love dance…a mating dance…

To a love song…

The Winter Day

The train cutting through the quiet, sleepy, winter vineyards.
The seldom seen winter sun, reflecting on the wet winter earth.
Glistening strips of sunlight resting on the dark, dull, brown ground.
The winter dew catching the light as it lines the fresh green grass.
Sparkly like lost tiny diamonds…. Bringing joy…

To the gray dull winter day…

Dawn

Look! As the dark, heavy, gray clouded sky hangs over the hidden, mystical, mossy green hills on this dull day.

A boat, asway to shore.
The winds, light, guiding the vessel softly to land.

A whale song soaked in the mighty sea, now aware to the present beauty.
The soft sweetness majestically rises from the depths,
crescendoing lovingly with the foamy white wave tips.

The waves wonderfully wander.

The solitary sleeping sun awaits…the changing season.

Wandering Boots

The snow has fallen the night before.
It lays crisp and fresh on the winter floor.
The sky brushed clear by gentle night breeze.
The sweet winter sun brightens this white blanket with ease.

The day is glorious, despite the cold.
She wraps herself up in woolens and winter boots of old.
Her mind drifts back to times forgotten and bold.
To a place in time when the bell tolled.

Her heart is filled with love and light,
to truly and finally feel alive.
The lantern-lit streets, the snowy feet,
the smiling children…rosy sweet.
Ladies and gentlemen, with carriages flowing,
through busy snowy streets…a-going.

The frozen forest floor, the swaying trees,
looking lovingly down on this village scene.
Both living together, side by side,
in union with each other, like groom and bride.
His collar stiffened tight, her long flowing frock,
softens his might, like a snow-covered rock.

Two times, two places, side by side.
The wanderer gets a glimpse while
time subsides…

Spirit on the Wind

Was taken briefly on the wind and spiraled among the trees.
The trees hath embraced me as their own.
Danced lightly among the leaves.
A while hath passed and taken was I to while among the mice.
Those little creatures with nests so sweet, nuzzled in the mother's chest.

Then traveled I over peaks of trees, with mockingbirds did rest,
And lay I over soft mossy land that I had named my bed.
And imagined I how I would feel if, one day, I were free.
Free to roam and free to fly and finally free to be.

But now I must take my weight and walk among the men.
But with me take I the lightness, which I gathered and shall pen.
The lightness I shall soak in words and pen of verse or two.
That verse shall swirl among the minds and remind them

of you.

The Hawthorn

Walking over hills and muddy fields,
I felt a weary feeling.
The wind called me to sit and rest underneath a hawthorn tree.
I sat beneath the dusky wood with radiant red berries overhead.
A little fairy did whisper to me, "Make a journey before you are dead."

I felt her voice upon the breeze, like childhood memories said.
"Listen to your dreams, my child, before your heart is bled.
Let your heart be strong, my child, and guide it with your life.
For troubled times are heading near, and there may be much strife.

So mind yourself, make your journey, and take care of your sweet life."
I listened well and thanked her kindly, although I did not know,
Where it was that she had meant that I would surely go…

It came to me in later year, the journey that was meant.
Was long ago written in time, and I would soon be sent.
The fairy that did come to me, I did meet a time or two.

The stories of which I will share with you,
When we have less to do.

Walking through the Falling Leaves

Walking through the falling leaves.
A wide straight path unfolds before me.
The golden red-brown leaves,
…once a coat for trees.

The fallen leaves pave my way.
The leaves fall and sway gently as I walk.
Some falling sooner and faster than others.
Some have fallen first, paving the way for their brothers.
Some falling later, composed, leaving their former home alone,
naked, and exposed.

Moving from one realm to the next.
From the glowing energetic emerald green,
to being dull, dead, and brown on the cold winter ground.
Lying, protecting, a warm moist coat for the mother…the earth.
Protecting the spring.
Young life yet to awaken…

The Daughters and Sons of Eve

The Daughters and Sons of Eve,
birthed and brought to a time of both turbulence and ease.
Tumbling through epochs of history.
Like a swirling journey through time and eternity.
Living and learning on this plane, this dramatic stage.
With many costumes and roles to play,
wars and lands to seize,
birthing of both kings and queens.
Moments of much meaning and moments with much of nothing.

This land changing, this creation taking,
many shapes with changing face.
With raging seas, high mountain peaks,
wide forests of trees, deep gorges, and canyons grand,
Earthquake-splitting grand this land and volcano-rolling lava rich.
For all to see.

Eve's children harnessing this wild and wondrous place.
Tilling, embracing, living, and dying.
Knowing much but knowing nothing.
Forgetting fro`m whence they came.
And now being beyond the pale.

Building, destroying, creating, flying, diving, exploring,
but somehow now ignoring the question at hand.

Why this land doth weep?
Why the sea's eyes send tears to the wide-open skies.
The mammoth towering trees, so old and wise,
sending wisdom on the breeze for all to hear and see.
They whisper, "Children of Eve, cast your loving ears to mountain
and beast, bird and tree, and listen to see what could indeed be the
remedy
in this swirling chaos.
Cast your wisdom, searching spirits, to the wide-open skies,
and listen to what is there to discover and receive."

Indeed, in following this lead, the children of Eve may well find,
with surprise, the ease they so long search,
to soothe all their needs.

About the Author

Jane Bauer was born in London, England, and grew up in Ireland. She studied nursing in England, then married and settled in south-western Germany. She loves spending time in nature and was inspired by the mystical forests of Germany to write her first poems.

She has, in recent years, moved to New Mexico, USA. There, Jane was further inspired by America's natural beauty, Native American culture, and our changing society to continue her poetic journey and create this collection of poems.

Eve a River Flowing is her first book.